30 DAYS TO
Taming
YOUR
Tongue

Deborah Smith Pegues

HARVEST HOUSE PUBLISHERS
EUGENE, OREGON

Cover by Koechel Peterson & Associates, Inc., Minneapolis, Minnesota

30 DAYS TO TAMING YOUR TONGUE
Copyright © 2005 by Deborah Smith Pegues
Published by Harvest House Publishers
Eugene, Oregon 97402
www.harvesthousepublishers.com

The Library of Congress has cataloged the edition as follows:

Pegues, Deborah Smith, 1950-
    30 days to taming your tongue / Deborah Smith Pegues.
        p. cm.
    Includes bibliographical references.
    ISBN 978-0-7369-1560-1 (pbk.)
    ISBN 978-0-7369-3430-5 (eBook)
    1. Oral communication—Religious aspects—Christianity. I. Title: Thirty days
    to taming your tongue. II. Title.

    BV4597.53.C64P44 2005
    248.4—dc22

                                                                    2004022177

Printed in the United States of America

13 14 15 16 17 18 19 / BP-MS / 43 42 41 40 39

Contents

Acknowledgments

It was through an incident with my friend Judge Mablean Ephriam of *Divorce Court TV* and her mature handling of one of my "mouth mess-ups" that I decided to enter an extended period of verbal abstinence, or what I called a "tongue fast." Yvonne Gibson Johnson, director of prayer at West Angeles Church in Los Angeles, California, insisted that God wanted me to share with others in the form of a book the lessons I learned during this period.

I also want to thank the following friends for their feedback and support: P. Bunny Wilson, Terri McFaddin, Mozetta Hillard, Michelle McKinney Hammond, Trina Jenkins, Dr. Judith McAllister, Delisa Kelley, Marilyn Beaubien, Nichole Palmer, Harold and Ruth Kelley, Gina Smith, and Charletta Benjamin.

My husband, Darnell Pegues, graciously sacrificed our time together to give me space to write. Thank you, sweetheart. There is no one like you in all the earth.

Prologue

Teachers often teach that which they need to learn themselves. I am no different. I am writing this book first and foremost for myself. I desire a wholesome tongue, one that always speaks what is pleasing to God. I have learned what James, the brother of Jesus, meant when he said, "No man can tame the tongue" (JAMES 3:8). Neither New Year's resolutions nor counting to ten nor other self-efforts will prevail in conquering this unruly member. To "tame" means to bring from a state of unruliness to a state of submission. A person would have to live in total isolation to begin to accomplish such a feat with his tongue. Even then, his self-talk would probably be negative in some way and therefore rob him of total victory.

The only hope for the tongue is the Spirit of God. The tongue must be bridled and brought into subjection by Him on a daily basis. How do we begin the process? One of my spiritual mentors gave me a very simple tip for dealing with the negative propensities of the natural man, or the "flesh." He said, "Whatever the flesh tells you to do, do the opposite." Well, that's a good place to start.

As you skimmed the list of the negative uses of the tongue in the table of contents, you may not have readily admitted that you are guilty of many of them. However, as you read this book with a desire to grow and to "own" behavior you may have been denying, you will experience the freedom that only comes with embracing the truth. "Ye shall know the truth, and the truth shall make you free" (JOHN 8:32 KJV). In this book I will challenge you to join me on a 30-day quest to become sensitive to the negative uses of the tongue and to "fast" or abstain from these verbal violations of godly principles.

Fasting, normally abstinence from food, is a spiritual discipline that few of God's people practice on a regular basis. After several incidents in which I realized I showed little or no verbal wisdom, I concluded that a strong resolve sustained by willpower alone was not going to bring me the victory. I vowed to set aside a time of tongue fasting.

Now, I want to caution that this book is not about turning you into a Passive Patsy or a Timid Tom who avoids expressing personal boundaries, desires, or displeasure with a situation. I have learned that most interpersonal problems will not be resolved without being confronted. However, there is a *time* and a *way* to say everything. We can rejoice knowing we are already empowered to use our tongues wisely.

> *The Lord GOD hath given me the tongue of*
> *the learned, that I should know how to speak*
> *a word in season* (ISAIAH 50:4 KJV).

Words are the *vehicle* through which we communicate our thoughts; the tongue is the *driver*. As such, it takes us to our destiny. Moving in spiritual maturity requires that we learn to speak the right words in the right season and for the right reason.

As the Holy Spirit sensitizes us to the negative uses of our tongue, we will begin to resist the temptation to drive down the wrong verbal path. If you find you are constantly at war with your tongue, I invite you to stop your harmful expressions. I guarantee you that at the end of this fast, you will become spiritually empowered as you transform your tongue into a wellspring of life.

Day 1

The Lying Tongue

The LORD detests lying lips,
but he delights in men who are truthful.

PROVERBS 12:22

Everything we do and say must be based upon the truth; lies make a shaky foundation for any relationship. Lying comes in four primary forms: deceitfulness, half-truths, exaggerations, and flattery. We will look at flattery in a separate chapter.

Deceitfulness

When I opened my mailbox and saw the letter from the Internal Revenue Service, my heart did not skip a beat as it had in the past. I used to dread those audits of my tax returns! Having been a faithful tither since the age of eighteen, I had learned over the years to keep a good record of my charitable giving because it usually generated an audit. However, I tended to be rather creative in interpreting the tax law in other aspects of the return. As I stood there fingering the envelope, I knew that, whatever the nature of the inquiry, all would be well, for I had support for all of the deductions taken. I couldn't help remembering a particular audit several years back in which I feigned ignorance of the tax law to justify my claim of a nondeductible educational expense. While sitting before the auditor and trying to appear innocent, I kept thinking, *God's going to strike me dead for lying!* All of my life, my Sunday school teachers had taught me that God had no tolerance for liars. Nevertheless, I had succumbed to the temptation of a larger tax refund. So there I sat, engaging in the most blatant form of lying—plain old deceitfulness. I decided then that life was too short to bear the anxiety and the remorse of being deceitful for a few extra dollars. Peter warns us, "Whoever would love life and see good days must keep his tongue from evil and his lips from deceitful speech" (1 PETER 3:10).

Why do some people practice deception? Many do it for financial gain, for social advantage, to hide immoral acts, or to obtain other "benefits." Jacob, whose name meant "trickster," conspired with his mother and deceived his father into giving him the birthright blessing that belonged to his brother Esau (GENESIS 27). When Esau discovered the deception, he threatened to kill him. Jacob was forced to leave town and to live with his Uncle Laban. Notwithstanding, he had to reap the seeds of deceit that he had sown. Laban tricked Jacob into marrying his daughter Leah, whom Jacob did not love. Laban further deceived Jacob by changing the terms of his employment agreement numerous times. Jacob was forced to work 14 years to marry Rachel, whom he did love. Eventually, because he abandoned his deceitful ways and became a tither, God blessed Jacob beyond his wildest imagination. He returned home after many years with a beautiful family, much abundance, and a new name: Israel.

Engaging in deceitfulness is a slap in God's face and has dire consequences. When we make a choice not to trust Him to handle a situation, we, in essence, decide He is a liar and will renege on His promise to meet every need. We then proceed to make our own way by any means necessary—even being deceptive. In doing so we forfeit the good life God had planned for us.

Half-Truths

Joan Smith took the day off on Monday. She returned to work on Tuesday and explained to her boss that she had been absent because her elderly mother had been hospitalized. The truth of the matter is that Joan had only spent two hours at the hospital and six hours shopping! Joan's objective was to have her boss believe that she had spent the entire day at her mother's bedside. She told a half-truth.

I was once the queen of half-truths and had convinced myself I was still walking in integrity. One of my favorite half-truths was blaming lost keys for my being late to an appointment. I seemed to always misplace my keys; however, I could usually locate them within a few minutes in one of several places I knew to look. The real reason for my tardiness was usually poor time management. When I would offer my excuse, I rationalized that the portion of my statement that I verbalized was true; I had indeed searched for the keys. But I ignored the fact that the undisclosed information, like the extra minutes I spent in the bed or my decision to complete an insignificant task, would have caused the hearer to draw a different conclusion about me. My husband finally impressed upon me the painful reality that *any* intent to deceive is a lie—period.

I find it interesting that the word "integrity" derives from "integer," which is a mathematical term. An integer is a whole number as opposed to a fraction. When we walk in integrity, we tell the whole truth and not just a fraction or part of it. Someone was well aware of the many ways there are to lie when he suggested that court oaths charge a person to tell "the truth, the whole truth, and nothing but the truth."

Exaggerating

Do you often embellish a story in order to get more attention from your listener? Exaggerating may seem harmless, but it is another form of lying. The danger in exaggerating is that those who are familiar with a person's propensity to stretch the truth will discount everything he says. This is also the paradox of exaggerating; a person stretches the truth to make something sound more believable, but then he loses his credibility because he exaggerates. I know several truth-stretchers. Their favorite words include absolute terms like "everybody," "nobody," and "always." Their friends jokingly warn, "Now, you know you should only believe about half of anything she says." What a terrible indictment. Is this how you would like to be viewed?

When you relate a story or an incident, know that it is okay to tell it with enthusiasm; just avoid the exaggerations. Stick to the facts at face value and resist the urge to be the center of attention by engaging in this form of lying.

God has sealed the destiny of every liar: "All liars shall have their part in the lake which burns with fire and brimstone, which is the second death" (REVELATION 21:8 NKJV). Death means separation. The first death is the separation of the spirit from the body; the second death is eternal separation of the spirit from God. Eternal separation from my Father is too high a price to pay for any form of deceitfulness.

The psalmist knew the consequences of deceitfulness and constantly implored God to keep him out of this pit. Consider his plea. "Deliver my soul, O LORD, from lying lips, and from a deceitful tongue" (PSALM 120:2 KJV). Have you been trusting God by telling the truth and leaving the consequences to Him, or do you need to join the psalmist in his prayer for deliverance?

TODAY'S AFFIRMATION:

"My mouth speaks what is true, for my lips detest wickedness. All the words of my mouth are just; none of them is crooked or perverse" (PROVERBS 8:7-8).

Day 2

The Flattering Tongue

*These people...flatter others
to get favors in return.*
JUDE 1:16 NLT

"How does it feel to be the most beautiful woman in the room?" According to an Internet poll of the best pickup lines, men voted this question as the most effective for flattering a woman.

Flattery is a lie covered in a bed of flowery words. Most people who engage in this dishonest communication do so to gain favor. The desired favor is not always something material or tangible; it can be an intangible benefit, such as acceptance. The flatterer may have low self-worth and believe others will like him if he compliments them.

Engaging in flattery is clear evidence of one's lack of faith in God's ability to give him favor with other people. Favor is a fringe benefit of being in right standing with our Creator.

> *For surely, O LORD, you bless the righteous;*
> *you surround them with your favor as with*
> *a shield* (PSALM 5:12).

There are many instances in the Bible of God giving His children favor with man—with no effort on their part. Consider that God gave Esther favor and the king chose her to be the queen of Persia (ESTHER 2). He gave Daniel favor with one of the king's officers, who allowed him and his three friends to select their own diet rather than eat the nonkosher food of their captors (DANIEL 1). God gave Joseph favor in Egypt, and he went from being a captive to commander of all the country's resources (GENESIS 39–41). These children of the Most High never had to resort to any form of self-effort in order to ingratiate themselves for gain or survival.

Can you think of a time that you flattered someone by giving him an insincere compliment? How did you feel afterward? Unless you have grown comfortable with such insincere behavior and have become insensitive to the Holy Spirit, flattering someone will most likely cause you to feel you have violated your personal integrity.

If you are a flatterer, understand that when you are over-complimenting a person, the flower of your words will soon wilt and lose all impact. Notwithstanding, if the person you chose to flatter is plagued with insecurity or has received little affirmation during her life, she will welcome any kind of attention that will bolster her low self-worth. There are periods in all of our lives when we may find ourselves vulnerable to flattery. These times can occur when we feel overlooked, unappreciated, unattractive, or a host of other negative emotions that Satan brings. I remember once when I attended a church where the opportunities to bring a message at a scheduled service were few and far between. On those rare occasions when I would speak, invariably a few people would come up to me and say that I was the most awesome speaker they had ever heard. They would go on to lament the fact that I did not get more opportunities to speak at the church. Now, I have to admit that hearing such accolades did indeed stroke my ego; however, I was quick to wonder if those persons were simply trying to ingratiate themselves with me or to get me to join them in their critical attitudes about the church.

Some people use flattery as a survival tactic. Story has it that movie director Steven Spielberg was the target of a bully's verbal and physical abuse when he was a skinny 13-year-old. Fed up with the constant harassment, one day Steven flattered the bully by telling him he looked like John Wayne and should consider playing the hero in an 8mm movie he was thinking of making about World War II. Once Steven outfitted him and cast him as a heroic squad leader, the bully was putty in his hands.*

Unlike Spielberg's bully, emotionally healthy people only appreciate sincere praise they earn for a specific distinction. Further, many can detect a compliment given to gain their favor as well as words spoken with ulterior motives. The paradox is that they will tend to look with disfavor, rather than favor, on someone who compliments them in general for no apparent reason.

Scripture is very clear on God's plans for the flatterer. "The LORD shall cut off all flattering lips..." (PSALM 12:3 KJV). Is flattery worth being cut off from the blessings of God?

—— TODAY'S AFFIRMATION: ——

"I will show partiality to no one, nor will I flatter any man; for if I were skilled in flattery, my Maker would soon take me away" (JOB 32:21-22).

---

* As cited at: www.anecdotage.com

Day 3

The Manipulating Tongue

Then Delilah pouted, "How can you say
you love me when you don't confide in me?
You've made fun of me three times now, and you
still haven't told me what makes you so strong!"

JUDGES 16:15 NLT

Samson was God's chosen man, but he had a pen-
chant for ungodly women. He was destined from
birth to play a vital role in liberating the Israelites
from the rule of the Philistines. God endowed him
with supernatural physical strength and cautioned
his parents that he was never to cut his hair, the secret
to his strength. Samson engaged in many exploits
that displayed his awesome muscle power; his enemies did not stand a chance against him.

Then he fell in love with a greedy, conniving
Philistine woman named Delilah. After many
attempts using the age-old, guilt-inducing "if you
love me, you would…" argument, she manipulated

Samson into telling her the secret to his great strength. Then, for financial gain, she betrayed his trust and revealed the mystery to his enemies. They promptly shaved his head and he became as weak as any other man. Having subdued him, they gouged out his eyes, bound him with chains, and forced him to grind in the prison. A broken and powerless man, Samson never regained his former glory.

One day during an event in which the Philistines were making sport of him, he stood between two temple pillars, prayed for one last infusion of super-natural strength, and literally brought the house down (see JUDGES 16). The collapsing structure killed him and more than 3000 spectators and government officials. This was the tragic end of a strong man who was weakened by a manipulative woman. Mani-pulation can destroy not only a relationship but also a person's life.

Today many men suffer from what I call "Delilah-phobia," the fear of disclosing their vulnerabilities. They have decided it is much safer to keep their weaknesses to themselves, rather than having the opposite sex use this sacred knowledge against them. Of course, their fear prevents them from achieving real intimacy with the opposite sex. It is critical that neither man nor woman should ever mention in a manipulative or retaliatory way their entrusted knowledge of the personal fears and weaknesses of another.

Manipulation is a crafty use of the tongue and a self-perpetuating vice. Once manipulators find that their craftiness helps them to achieve their objectives, they become proud of their "smooth operating" skills. They will use all kinds of indirect tactics ranging from "guilt trips" to portraying themselves as innocent, suffering victims of various circumstances. They may even start to enjoy their ability to influence others in such a manner. Why, I have heard men boast, "I can get a woman to do anything!"

While manipulators are subtle and make every attempt to cloak their self-serving motives, they often forget that many people are very discerning and have a keen sensitivity to such insincerity. Further, manipulators lose all credibility once people become aware of their propensity to engage in such behavior. People will suspect that they always have ulterior motives and will avoid them like the plague.

Some people are bold enough to confront manipulators and to call their motives into question. Jesus did so when His enemies sent spies to Him posing as sincere religious people. The spies were to manipulate Him into speaking against the Roman government. They attempted to flatter Him by complimenting His integrity and His impartiality. Then they asked the question they thought would surely be self-incriminating and land Him in jail: "'Is it lawful for us to pay taxes to Caesar or not?' But He perceived their craftiness, and said to them, 'Why do you test Me?'" (LUKE 20:22-23 NKJV). He proceeded to explain that they should give to Caesar, the Roman emperor, whatever belonged to him and to give to God what was due to Him. He refused to be a victim of their manipulation. Further, we never read of Jesus manipulating anybody. He always offered everyone a better way of life but accepted their decision to pursue another option even when it was not in their best interest.

It would behoove us to emulate Him in this regard. Manipulation is deceptive and attempts to take away a person's freewill choice. God's children must not practice nor tolerate such behavior.

TODAY'S AFFIRMATION:

Because I am in right standing with God, He surrounds me with favor. Therefore, I have no need to manipulate anyone for personal gain or advantage.

The Hasty Tongue

Do you see a man hasty in his words?
There is more hope for a fool than for him.
PROVERBS 29:20 NKJV

Do you sometimes offend others because you do not engage your brain before shifting your tongue into drive? Have you ever made a commitment to God or man without giving it much consideration and later reneged on it? The communication of the hasty tongue is done too quickly to be thoughtful or wise.

Offending in Haste

No matter how holy we are, we will eventually offend somebody because of hasty speech. "For in many things we offend all. If any man offend not in word, the same is a perfect man, and able also to bridle the whole body" (JAMES 3:2 KJV). Because we can never be totally aware of all of the sensitivities of

25

others, we must depend upon the Holy Spirit to direct our speech in a way that does not tap into their pain, distress, or other negative experiences. I have seen people innocently offend others in an attempt to interject humor into a situation. We must realize that everyone has a different sensitivity level depending upon his experiences. I try to practice not being easily offended and often give others the benefit of the doubt when they make a hasty remark I might otherwise find offensive.

Responding in Haste

The Bible cautions, "He who answers before listening—that is his folly and his shame" (PROVERBS 18:13). I once had an employee who responded to my inquiries so hastily that he did not take time to understand what I was really asking. His fear of failure and his need to establish his worth were so great that he felt compelled to answer quickly to prove he was adequate. Thus, his answer was usually irrelevant to the question. How frustrating! His actions caused me to view him the very way he was trying so hard to avoid.

Committing in Haste

God does not want us to be flaky. He expects us to keep our promises. In the book of Ecclesiastes,

Solomon warns us against making a hasty, ill-considered vow to the Lord. "Do not be rash with your mouth, and let not your heart utter anything hastily before God" (ECCLESIASTES 5:2 NKJV). He goes on to explain that we should not try to wiggle out of our commitment by saying that it was a mistake.

Jephthah learned a lesson on the folly of a hasty vow the hard way—through experience (JUDGES 11:30-40). When he led the Israelites to war against the Ammonites, he vowed that if God gave him the victory, he would sacrifice to the Lord the first thing that came out of his house upon his return. Little did he know that it would be his only daughter. Scripture is not clear as to whether he sacrificed her on an altar of fire (contrary to God's laws) or whether she was doomed to be a virgin the rest of her life. However he fulfilled his vow, his daughter was negatively impacted because of his hasty commitment.

Seeing that I was plagued by the malady of hasty speech, a mentor admonished me, "Stop, think, and pray before you speak." James, the Lord's brother, said it best. "Wherefore, my beloved brethren, let every man be swift to hear, slow to speak" (JAMES 1:19 KJV). Have you ever wondered why God gave us two ears and one mouth? Perhaps we are to spend twice as much time listening than talking. A good pause would serve us well in the long run. Time and words are two things that, once gone, can never be recovered. We must take time to weigh our words before we release them.

TODAY'S AFFIRMATION:

I am swift to hear and slow to speak. The Lord has set a guard over my mouth and He keeps watch over the door of my lips.

Day 5

The Divisive Tongue

Blessed are the peacemakers:
for they shall be called the children of God.
MATTHEW 5:9 KJV

Divide and conquer is one of Satan's most effective strategies for hindering the effectiveness of any effort undertaken by two or more people. He knows the power, synergy, and blessings that result when we work in harmony; therefore, he makes every effort to bring division.

Sometimes it is hard to believe there are people who deliberately engage in bringing dissension. I had a cousin who had experienced much domestic turmoil during her childhood. Years later at our family gatherings, she was not satisfied until she had picked a fight or maneuvered somebody into an argument with another person. Being a "peace-breaker" seemed to make her happier than enjoying family camaraderie. Dissension and division were so ingrained in her that she embraced them as normal. She professed a relationship with God, but her behavior overshadowed her claim.

The sixth chapter of Proverbs lists seven things that the Lord detests; among them is "a man who stirs up dissension among brothers" (VERSE 19). In Ephesians 4:3, Paul urges believers to keep the "unity of the Spirit through the bond of peace." Obviously, he knew that keeping peace required tremendous effort. We cannot afford to be ignorant of Satan's tactics to keep us at odds. He will cause us to become offended over a harmless statement, to read more meaning into a comment than the speaker intended, to ascribe impure motives to someone's behavior, or to believe a lie. Oh, that we would practice being more discerning! The Holy Spirit will surely reveal the truth of a situation. He is our peace, and when we embrace Him, He directs us into peaceful resolutions of our issues. In fact, our conflicts can become stepping-stones to stronger relationships when we make a commitment to understand each other and to refrain from divisiveness.

Have you used your tongue to sow discord? Know that anytime you tell another person something negative that someone else has said about him, your action will probably cause division. This is not to say you should avoid warning a person about another who is not acting in his best interests. However, you must be honest about your underlying motive. You may be trying to gain that person's favor by appearing loyal enough to expose the bad guy, or you may be indirectly communicating your own feelings about the person at the expense of another. Whatever your rationale, the result is still the same—a relationship will be damaged and God will be displeased. As you recall the last time you used your tongue as a tool of divisiveness, consider what excuse you used for doing so. Are you ready to repent for this sin?

Not only are we to refrain from causing division, we must also become active agents of peace, using our best efforts to reconcile parties in conflict.

TODAY'S AFFIRMATION:

I will make every effort to speak words that engender peace and to refrain from any communication that creates disunity.

Day 6

The Argumentative Tongue

Avoiding a fight is a mark of honor;
only fools insist on quarreling.

PROVERBS 20:3 NLT

Unlike divisive people, whose actions destroy unity between parties, argumentative people enjoy directly resisting anyone whose viewpoint is different from theirs. In fact, they seem to stay on high alert for anything they can discuss that will get someone else on the defensive. Never without fodder for a verbal fight, they can always depend upon any discussion of religion or politics to produce unending quarrels.

Being argumentative is a futile use of the tongue and certainly not the way to win friends or influence people. It was legendary American-cowboy-turned-entertainer Will Rogers who cautioned, "People's minds are changed through observation and not through argument." In other words, contentiousness negates one's ability to bring about change.

Let's look at why people become quarrelers.

Many quarrelers grew up in homes where arguing was as much a pattern as eating. Thus, they think it is normal to contend. I grew up in a very contentious environment. I don't remember any discussions ever ending in an amicable resolution of the initial issue. Rather, it seemed that when the quarrelers could not find more logs to put on the fire at hand, they simply kindled another fire and continued the process until they tired of talking. I swore I would never engage in such ineffective communication. On the other hand, I have a brother who always tries to draw people into discussions that often result in an argument. When he runs out of points to put forth or has no logical response to his opponents' rebuttals, he resorts to personal attacks on their character and name-calling. He has chosen to emulate the behavior he witnessed as a child.

Another reason some people resort to quarreling is to bolster their own self-worth. They can only feel good about themselves by attacking the validity of other people's opinions, philosophies, or beliefs and then maneuvering them into defending their position. The quarreler's goal is not to add value to someone's life by showing him the error of his way. In fact, Mrs. Quarreler would be greatly disappointed if her target responded, "Oh, thank you for shedding light on this matter. I will change my thinking immediately." Why, such a concession would end the argument!

I have decided it is best to heed Solomon's advice: "Beginning a quarrel is like opening a floodgate, so drop the matter before a dispute breaks out" (PROVERBS 17:14 NLT). When engaged by a quarreler, my favorite response is to say early on, with as much finality as I can muster, "Okay. That's your opinion." This will keep me out of the web of contention that quarrelers are expert at weaving. It takes two to tangle. Jesus cautioned us to "agree with your adversary quickly" (MATTHEW 5:25 NKJV).

Most people, except fellow quarrelers, will minimize or avoid discussion with a person who is argumentative. They find it too stressful to walk on eggshells trying to limit their conversations to safe, non-debatable topics.

One of the challenges for God's children is to learn to disagree without being disagreeable. We glorify God when we remain loving even when we disagree with the views and values of unbelievers. We must be careful how we disagree lest we compromise our testimony. Surely we have the grace to register our protests without being mean-spirited. Benjamin

Franklin was known to remark diplomatically, "On this point, I agree. But on the other, if you don't mind, may I take exception?"

If you have a tendency to be contentious or argumentative, remember that it costs you absolutely nothing to respect someone's opinion—especially on matters that have no eternal consequences.

TODAY'S AFFIRMATION:

I will resist becoming contentious by respecting everyone's right to have his own values and views.

Day 7

The Boasting Tongue

Let another praise you, and not your own mouth;
someone else, and not your own lips.

PROVERBS 27:2

Are you so proud of your accomplishments or
your possessions that you cannot help but boast
about them? Boasting implies that your good for-
tune is a result of your own efforts. Have you for-
gotten that everything you have came from God?
King Nebuchadnezzar did. One day, as he was
strolling on the roof of his palace, he had a conversation with himself that would change the rest of his
life.

> *As he looked out across the city, he said, "Just*
> *look at this great city of Babylon! I, by my*
> *own mighty power, have built this beautiful*
> *city as my royal residence and as an expres-*
> *sion of my royal splendor"* (DANIEL 4:30
> NLT).

Scripture tells us that God interrupted Nebu-chadnezzar's proud moment and declared to him that he would lose his kingdom immediately! He was driven from the palace and forced to live as a common derelict. His hair grew like the feathers of an eagle and his nails like the claws of a bird. He even became mentally ill. It was not until he acknowledged God as the ruler over everything that God gave him back his sanity and restored his kingdom. Hear his testimony:

> *At the end of that time, I, Nebuchadnezzar, raised my eyes toward heaven, and my sanity was restored. Then I praised the Most High; I honored and glorified him who lives forever. His dominion is an eternal domin-ion; his kingdom endures from generation to generation. All the peoples of the earth are regarded as nothing. He does as he pleases with the powers of heaven and the peoples of the earth. No one can hold back his hand or say to him: "What have you done?"* (DANIEL 4:34-35).

We must learn to consciously take the backseat when pride screams for the front row. Study the fate of proud men in the Bible. Meditate on Scriptures that deal with humility and pride. I have framed the passage below and keep it in my view in my office.

> *Who makes you different from anyone else?*
> *What do you have that you did not receive?*
> *And if you did receive it, why do you boast*
> *as though you did not?* (1 CORINTHIANS
> 4:7).

Whatever skills or talents God has given to you, they are for His glory. Learn to take praise in stride. If your popularity increases, don't be intoxicated by the accolades. Remember that praise is like perfume. If you consume it, it will kill you!

TODAY'S AFFIRMATION:

"By the grace of God, I am what I am"
(1 CORINTHIANS 15:10).

Day 8

The Self-Deprecating Tongue

*Moses said to the LORD, "O Lord, I have
never been eloquent, neither in the past
nor since you have spoken to your servant.
I am slow of speech and tongue."*

EXODUS 4:10

You engage in self-deprecation when you think
or speak of yourself as being of little or no worth and
thereby minimize the value of what you "bring to
the table" or have to offer. Notice how Satan seeks
to take us from one extreme to the other. He tries
to make us either boastful or bashful. He tries to
make us think that we are "da bomb" (slang for
"really hot stuff") or "done bombed" (totally blew
it!). Don't be ignorant of his tricks.

Self-deprecation is often disguised as humility;
but in reality, it is a rejection of the Word of God,

which assures us we can do all things through Christ who strengthens us (PHILIPPIANS 4:13). Watch those negative labels you put on yourself. What others call you is not important; it is only what you call yourself.

Consider the account of Jesus and the man who had been possessed by demons for a very long time. "Jesus asked him, saying, What is thy name? And he said, Legion: because many devils were entered into him" (LUKE 8:30 KJV). A "legion" was a major unit of the Roman army consisting of up to 6000 troops; "Legion" was not this man's given name. Being possessed by a legion of demons was a temporary condition he had come to accept as permanent reality. He had dealt with the problem for so long that he labeled or defined himself by his experience.

Have you had an experience that you have allowed to define you? Perhaps you have labeled yourself a "fatso" because you have battled your weight for a long time with no apparent victory in sight. Alternatively, maybe you have defined yourself as a "victim" because you were truly victimized more than once. You may even consider yourself a "failure" because you are divorced. It is time to abandon the negative labels and redefine yourself!

Self-deprecation displeases God. When Moses complained that he was inadequate to lead the Israelites out of Egyptian bondage because of his speech impediment, God became upset.

> The LORD said to him, "Who gave man his mouth? Who makes him deaf or mute? Who gives him sight or makes him blind? Is it not I, the LORD? Now go; I will help you speak and will teach you what to say" (EXODUS 4:11-12).

What an awesome promise from an Omnipotent Being who cannot lie. We must reject the spirit of inadequacy. Without God, we can do nothing anyway; with Him we can do all things. Because of the reality of His Word, we can walk in confidence—not in ourselves—but in the grace of God that empowers us.

TODAY'S AFFIRMATION:

God is able to make *all* grace abound toward me; so that I *always* having *all* sufficiency in *all things,* may abound to *every* good work.

Day 9

The Slandering Tongue

To hide hatred is to be a liar;
to slander is to be a fool.
PROVERBS 10:18 NLT

Slanderers make malicious, false, or even true
statements about others with the intent of damaging
their reputation, character, or good name. Political
campaigners are notorious for releasing slanderous
statements to the media with the hope of disadvan-
taging their opponents. Rare is the candidate who
runs a totally clean campaign these days. Slandering
is not limited to politicians, however. Given certain
circumstances, anyone can be tempted to denigrate
another. One thing that we can be assured of is that
there won't be any slanderers in heaven.

> LORD, who may dwell in your sanctuary?
> Who may live on your holy hill? He whose
> walk is blameless and who does what is
> righteous, who speaks the truth from his

heart and has no slander on his tongue, who
does his neighbor no wrong and casts no slur
on his fellowman (PSALM 15:1-3).

Can you recall a time in which you made detracting remarks about someone? What was your motive in doing so? Why did you feel the need to diminish that person's character in the eyes of another? Were you speaking out of the pain of being hurt by her? Did you envy her accomplishments? If so, have you not learned how to let your envy motivate you to achieve your own goals rather than cause you to defame another? It is likely you grudgingly admire and desire something that the other person possesses.

Some people are so insecure and easily threatened that they feel they must cast aspersions on the character of others whom they perceive as "the competition" in order to maintain their position. Such was the case of Diotrephes, a New Testament church leader. He found himself in a real dilemma when John recommended some anointed teachers of the gospel to speak at his church. Plagued with insecurity, he feared that their visit would threaten his preeminence, so he refused to allow them to come. John was quite upset with his behavior and explained to his friend Gaius how he planned to deal with it.

> *When I come, I will report some of the things*
> *he is doing and the wicked things he is saying*
> *about us. He not only refuses to welcome the*
> *traveling teachers, he also tells others not to*
> *help them. And when they do help, he puts*
> *them out of the church* (3 JOHN 1:10 NLT).

You can find many a Diotrephes in sacred and secular organizations. They cast aspersions on threatening newcomers; they accuse bright, talented women of getting ahead by means other than skills, talents, and qualifications. They look for a chink in their victim's armor. Contrary to what they think, diminishing the image of another is not going to enhance their image.

Resorting to slander is clear evidence that one has not embraced certain of God's promises. For instance, because of Psalm 75:6-7, I know for certain that promotions and exaltation come from God rather than man. This truth causes me to be a team player. There is no reason for me to snuff out anybody's light so that mine will shine. Further, God has declared that no man can thwart His purpose for our lives.

> *The LORD Almighty has spoken—who can*
> *change his plans? When his hand moves,*
> *who can stop him?* (ISAIAH 14:27 NLT).

Since God has secured our destiny and has promised to avenge all wrongs perpetrated against us, why engage in slander? I find it interesting that the Greek word for "slander" is derived from *diabolos,* which means "devil." Slandering is an illegal, diabolical act that God abhors. When we attempt to defame others with our denigrating words, we are sowing evil seeds for which we will surely reap the consequences. "He who guards his mouth preserves his life, but he who opens wide his lips shall have destruction" (PROVERBS 13:3 NKJV).

TODAY'S AFFIRMATION:

I refuse to be a slanderer. I will use Philippians 4:8 as my conversation sifter. Therefore, whatever things are true, noble, just, pure, lovely, and of good report, if there is any virtue and if there is anything praiseworthy about someone, I comment only on these things.

Day 10

The Gossiping Tongue

The words of a gossip are like choice morsels;
they go down to a man's inmost parts.

PROVERBS 18:8

It seemed that every woman at the beauty shop had an opinion about why Oprah Winfrey had not married her longtime beau, Stedman Graham. Refusing to join the discussion, I buried my head in my book and decided it was a good time to catch up on my reading. Because I have been the subject of a few "newsy" conversations, I have an aversion to such nonproductive exchanges. I sat there thinking, *What's it to you? Why do you care?*

Do you sometimes engage in idle and often malicious talk about the personal affairs of another? Gossip can be such a delectable "choice morsel" that many find it impossible to resist. Now, I'm certain everyone reading this book has been guilty of partaking of this popular pastime—either as a bearer or a hearer at one time or another. Oh, the downside of such behavior!

Did you know that gossiping can lower your sense of self-worth? How? When you gossip, you tend to realize you are not walking in integrity. We feel best about ourselves when we do things that are pleasing to God; after all, He created us for His pleasure.

What's the solution? How do you stop gossiping? Catch yourself before you indulge! Ask yourself why you are being a bearer of such news. Is this the only way you know how to establish camaraderie with others? Do you need to be the center of attention? Does it make you feel superior to know something negative about somebody that the hearer doesn't know? Are you envious of your subject's accomplishments? Why are you willing to use the temple of God as a "trash receptacle" by being a receiver of gossip? What do you plan to do with the information a gossip shares with you? Are you bored with your life and need more meaningful activities? It has been my observation that those who are ardently pursuing their own goals and aspirations are less likely to waste time discussing the affairs of another.

If you are serious about eliminating gossip from your life, you must start an all-out campaign against it. Let everyone know you will not be a bearer or a hearer of "choice morsels" about anyone. Declare your environment, whether at work, at home, or at play, to be a "gossip-free zone." Make every effort to avoid gossipmongers. Proverbs 20:19 warns, "A gossip tells secrets, so don't hang around with someone who talks too much" (NLT).

When people come into my office and start to gossip or to engage in any other ungodly talk, I point to my tongue and exclaim, "tongue fast!" They immediately know I have no plans to indulge their conversation. Refusing to engage in gossip may result in fewer visitors and phone calls; however, your impact will be far-reaching. I have received emails, calls, and letters from people across the United States testifying about the impact that the tongue fast is having on their lives.

When your tongue is used as an instrument of righteousness, your stock will rise in heaven. You will be able to humbly declare, with complete dependence on the Father, "Let the words of my mouth, and the meditation of my heart, be acceptable in thy sight, O LORD, my strength, and my redeemer" (PSALM 19:14 KJV).

TODAY'S AFFIRMATION:

I am not a busybody in other people's matters. Therefore, I do not yield my tongue as an instrument of gossip.

The Meddling Tongue

*Some of you are living idle lives,
refusing to work and wasting time
meddling in other people's business.*

2 THESSALONIANS 3:11 NLT

"Nosey Rosey" is the label that the people in my hometown placed on those who were always prying into or meddling in the affairs of others. While mothers-in-law have the reputation for being prime meddlers, they have not cornered the market on this vice. Men, relatives, coworkers, and well-meaning friends are also prone to prying from time to time.

Unlike gossips, meddlers usually seek personal information directly from their subjects. "How can you afford such an expensive item?" "What size is the dress you're wearing?" "How much did you pay for this house?" "How long can you afford to be off from work?" These are the types of questions that serve no other purpose than to satisfy an inquiring mind. In all fairness, not everyone who makes inquiries is meddling. Many are sincerely interested in helping others.

Whether you are genuinely concerned or just plain curious, be especially careful to avoid probing questions when conversing with those who are ill. "What did the doctor say about your condition?" Bad question. It is best to wait for someone to volunteer detailed information about his personal health.

If you are prone to natural curiosity, you must make a special effort to keep your inquisitiveness within the bounds of what is socially and spiritually appropriate. In some situations you may have no intentions of prying; however, you may still run the risk of your inquisitiveness offending others.

My husband hates nosiness. I have to remind him to be gracious in responding to queries about the price of his personal purchases, such as a car or any of his recreational "toys." He will often respond, "Are you planning to buy one?" When someone questions me about the price of something, I will usually offer a wide price range or jokingly say "somewhere between one hundred and a million dollars." I try to be mindful of the fact that some individuals—and even people of certain cultures—do not know that others deem their queries as nosiness. Usually a simple response such as, "I'm sorry, that's confidential" or "That's personal" will be sufficient to stop further probing.

The Bible offers an interesting perspective on meddling: "He who passes by and meddles in a quarrel not his own is like one who takes a dog by the ears" (PROVERBS 26:17 NKJV). A dog's ears are one of the most sensitive parts of his body; if you pull them, he may bite you. Likewise, when we stick our noses where they do not belong, we may get a negative response. I have learned this from personal experience. I had a relative who found herself in dire financial straits. At her request, we sat together for several hours and developed a plan for paying off her debts and getting her back on track. Later, I helped to orchestrate a deal that yielded her a significant sum of money. When I reminded her to follow the plan we had established, she became offended by what she perceived as my intrusion into her business. She reminded me that she was not a child and could manage her affairs just fine! I was devastated, for I knew I had pure motives with no intentions of meddling. The moral of the story is, even if you feel you have earned the right to stick your nose into a situation, walk softly. You might want to pray about it first and leave the matter to God. He is always better at influencing circumstances than we are.

If you are a parent, some meddling is certainly in order to keep your inexperienced, live-at-home children from going down the wrong path. Don't be afraid of their negative attitudes or their rejection. In the final analysis, most of them will appreciate your intervention. If your children have reached adulthood, try to accept the fact that grown-ups do not need parenting. The law of sowing and reaping the consequences of bad decisions is still one of the most effective teachers of life's lessons. Give them space to learn.

If you are indeed a genuine meddler, know that God does not consider your nose-poking a small matter. He classifies this sin—yes, *sin*—with murder and stealing.

> *If you suffer, however, it must not be for murder, stealing, making trouble, or prying into other people's affairs* (1 PETER 4:15 NLT).

When tempted to meddle, why not engage in a little self-interrogation? Ask yourself, "Do I have a sincere, unselfish motive for prying into this matter, or am I attempting to control things for my desired objectives?" Someone once said that one reason why people who mind their own business are successful is that they have so little competition. Think about that!

—— TODAY'S AFFIRMATION ——

I am genuinely interested in others and only seek information from them that will allow me to serve, love, and support them better.

Day 12

The Betraying Tongue

A gossip betrays a confidence,
but a trustworthy man keeps a secret.

PROVERBS 11:13

Betrayal is a more blatant act than gossip. A gossip may not necessarily harbor any ill will toward his victim; however, a betrayer divulges information in breach of a confidence. He gives information to the "enemy" and commits relational treason by violating the trust someone has placed in him. This ungodly use of the tongue is designed to hurt or disadvantage.

Judas was able to betray Jesus with very little effort because he was familiar with His comings and goings.

> *Now Judas, who betrayed him, knew the place, because Jesus had often met there with his disciples* (JOHN 18:2).

Judas used his inside knowledge of Jesus' habits to hurt Him. Later, his betrayal caused Judas such self-loathing that he committed suicide. Such an act must surely eat away at one's self-esteem and sense of dignity. Have you ever betrayed someone's confidence? Be honest. Why did you do it? What was your payoff? Did you gain some advantage because of it? Were you feeling envious at the time? Was there an unresolved conflict between the two of you? Have you repented for this sin?

On the other hand, has someone betrayed your confidence? Were you reaping what you had sown? What valuable lesson did you learn from the incident? Have you released the offender in your heart and no longer desire vengeance? If not, you are still bound to him and he is still controlling your life. Let it go. God saw the betrayal *before* it happened and *while* it was happening. Since He chose not to intervene, accept it as part of His sovereign plan for your life. Learn from the burn, but forgive to live. Remind yourself that in the final analysis, the incident will work together for your good because you love God and are called according to His purpose (ROMANS 8:28).

Decide today to strive to be a trustworthy person whom others can depend upon to guard their secrets.

If you are blessed to have a trustworthy friend, thank God for such a rare jewel.

TODAY'S AFFIRMATION:

I am a trustworthy person and can be depended upon to keep a confidence.

Day 13

The Belittling Tongue

Do not let any unwholesome talk come out
of your mouths, but only what is helpful for
building others up according to their needs,
that it may benefit those who listen.

EPHESIANS 4:29

Do people feel better about themselves after spending time with you? Or are your expectations so high that you focus on their shortcomings rather than their assets? If someone speaks well of a person you envy, do you follow up with a disparaging remark? Are you so insecure that you can only feel good about yourself by denigrating others? "Therefore encourage one another and build up one another, just as you also are doing" (1 THESSALONIANS 5:11 NASB).

When we had a room expanded at our home, I was fascinated by the use of the hammer. It was used in the demolition as well as the construction process.

Words are like that. They can tear down or they can build. How do you use your words mostly? Is it your normal behavior to build?

During your tongue fast, conquer belittling by acting as if you are a cheerleader and a coach to your family members, employees, coworkers, and others in your sphere of interaction. Cheerleaders tell you that you can do it; coaches tell you how to reach the goal. They all have the same goal: They want you to win!

Now, I know from experience that if you tend to be one of those hard-driving, goal-oriented people, coaching may be a challenge initially. Perhaps you are from the school of thought that believes an employee's paycheck is encouragement enough—especially if he is more than adequately compensated. Beware! Thou art stuck in the stone ages and in dire need of a mindset change. If you want to maximize productivity, then learn how to build up your employees. I have found that it is not my natural inclination to want to coach poor performers; I just want them out. In with the new superstars! What I have learned is that a little positive affirmation, some hand-holding, and lots of communication will often yield the productivity and the loyalty that may not accompany the cocky superstar.

Make it a habit to affirm your family members and friends. Tell your wife she is the only woman for you, express your appreciation for your husband's sense of responsibility, applaud your teenager for avoiding drugs and alcohol, thank a friend for keeping your secrets! Resist the temptation to constantly "fix" something about them. Accept them as they are and remember that you only have them for a season.

TODAY'S AFFIRMATION:

No unwholesome talk comes out of my mouth, but only what is helpful for building others up according to their needs, that it may benefit those who listen.

Day 14

The Cynical Tongue

Blessed is the man that walketh not in the counsel
of the ungodly, nor standeth in the way of sinners,
nor sitteth in the seat of the scornful.

PSALM 1:1 KJV

Eliab, David's oldest brother, was a true cynic. When David went down to the scene of the battle and saw Goliath, the Philistine giant who was intimidating the Israelites, he became indignant. He emphatically and confidently stated that he would personally take care of this "uncircumcised Philistine" (1 SAMUEL 17:36). Circumcision was a sign of God's covenant of protection and provision for the Israelites. David knew that this bully had no such covenant with God; only the Israelites could claim such a benefit. David was very secure in the covenant and totally embraced God's promise. Obviously, this was not so for Eliab.

Now Eliab his oldest brother heard when he
spoke to the men; and Eliab's anger burned

> *against David and he said, "Why have you*
> *come down? And with whom have you left*
> *those few sheep in the wilderness? I know*
> *your insolence and the wickedness of your*
> *heart; for you have come down in order to*
> *see the battle." But David said, "What have*
> *I done now?"* (1 SAMUEL 17:28-29 NASB).

Eliab, whose name meant "God is my father" (imagine one with such a name running from the giant), scorned David's confidence and his motives; cynicism had him in its grip.

A person who is cynical scorns the motives of others. Cynicism is like venom; it poisons the atmosphere wherever it is present. Resorting to it will also poison your spirit and that of others. Find one cynical employee, parishioner, or family member, and pretty soon those with weaker minds are chiming in and perpetuating the negative conversation. It can wreak havoc on any relationship and in any environment. When I managed a staff of people who were always under the gun to complete important deadlines, I tried to reward and de-stress them by taking the entire staff to lunch from time to time. Because this required us to close our department for a couple of hours, attendance was mandatory. There was one antisocial sourpuss, however, who always put a damper on our outings with her cynical remarks and overall negative attitude about the company. I finally started letting her stay at the office while the rest of us had a good time. I found that distancing myself from a cynic was my best coping strategy.

As you proceed on your tongue fast, really begin to observe your comments in various settings and determine if you are being cynical or scornful. Retire from cynicism today.

TODAY'S AFFIRMATION:

I am blessed because I do not walk in the counsel of the ungodly nor stand in the way of sinners nor sit in the seat of the scornful.

Day 15

The Know-It-All Tongue

A prudent man conceals knowledge.
PROVERBS 12:23 NASB

Are you so all-knowing that you cannot refrain from giving unsolicited input? Do you have an unusually high regard for your opinion? Do you regularly use the expression, "You should...?" Please allow me to gently remind you that most emotionally healthy people will resent someone who always assumes he knows what is best for them. We must give people the benefit of the doubt in pursuing an independent course of action. Even if you feel you have earned the right to speak into someone's life or to give unsolicited advice, proceed with caution. "Have you considered...?" sounds a lot less controlling and will be more welcomed—especially by men—than "You should..." Married women, take heed! Real men aren't looking for Mother. Right before I got married, one of my spiritual mentors gave me a bit of advice. "We know you're smart," she cautioned, "but don't know everything. Let your husband know some things sometimes." I have heeded this simple wisdom for more than a quarter of a century with good results.

Even if you have knowledge and insight into a certain situation, sometimes it's prudent to keep silent and give another the joy and fulfillment of explaining it to you. "Wise people don't make a show of their knowledge" (PROVERBS 12:23 NLT). Assuming the role of the arrogant expert on almost every topic is a sure indication of pride, which is repulsive behavior to God and man.

How do you let go of that know-it-all tongue? You can start by letting someone share information with you that you already know—without letting him know that you know it. This can be great training in humility and emotional maturity. Often, when my husband and I are about to make a large purchase, such as a car, I chuckle within as the salesperson, usually a male, assumes I know nothing about finances. He proceeds to explain loan terms and other financial aspects of the deal. I go with the flow and watch his astonishment when he finds out that I am a certified public accountant with many years of experience. Of course, my husband stands there fighting the temptation to yell, "She already knows that!" I do it simply for practice in maintaining humility.

Even if you are brilliant but humble, your mere presence may cause those with low self-esteem to feel inferior. Certainly, then, displaying intellectual superiority will alienate others. Some people may look for areas of weakness to "cut you down to size."

If you tend to be a know-it-all, maybe you need to do a little honest introspection. Is your display of knowledge a smoke screen for insecurity? Are you craving attention or appreciation because you are not getting it from the source you desire? When interacting with a group, you might want to actively listen to others, ask for their ideas, resist correcting or contradicting anybody, and limit your input to only one or two points. Your interpersonal relationships will improve when people feel that interacting with you has been a mutual sharing of ideas.

TODAY'S AFFIRMATION:

I am prudent and therefore I do not flaunt my knowledge.

Day 16

The Harsh Tongue

A gentle answer turns away wrath, but a harsh word stirs up anger.

PROVERBS 15:1

In my impatience and frustration with incompetence or low productivity in others, I have sometimes made what some felt were harsh remarks. When I have worked in a company culture where termination for poor performance was rare, I felt that telling the employee the harsh truth was my only recourse. This imprudent use of my tongue has never yielded positive results.

Solomon says of the wise woman in the book of Proverbs, "She opens her mouth with wisdom, and on her tongue is the law of kindness" (PROVERBS 31:26 NKJV). Speaking kindly to others was one of the core principles of this woman's life. When you really think about it, there is never any justification for being harsh or unkind in our communication. If we claim that God is our Father, we won't practice such behavior either. We will deliberately choose words that are warmhearted, understanding, and sympathetic. As a steward of the grace God has extended to us, we must in turn extend that same grace to others. We must cultivate the habit of speaking kind words especially to those whom we feel may not deserve it—isn't that what grace is all about? Caution! This does not mean that we are to bury our heads in the sand and refuse to deal with problematic situations. However, before we approach anyone, we must go to God and get His words, which always get the desired results. "So is my word that goes out from my mouth: It will not return to me empty, but will accomplish what I desire and achieve the purpose for which I sent it" (ISAIAH 55:11). We cannot achieve God's purpose while being harsh.

There are various degrees of harshness, with verbal abuse being at the extreme end of the spectrum. The old saying, "Sticks and stones may break my bones, but words can never harm me" is totally untrue. Harsh words never die, and they can impact a person for a lifetime. Many who are considered society's outcasts today have been victims of verbal abuse at some point during their lives. Their perpetrators include parents, teachers, insecure spouses, and others who may have been battling their own emotional issues. If you find that you are prone to speaking harshly when angry, begin to seek God for deliverance. Whatever it takes, including enrolling in anger management classes, do it. Solomon said, "He who is slow to anger is better than the mighty, and he who rules his spirit than he who takes a city" (PROVERBS 16:32 NKJV). You can begin to take control over that destructive behavior by the power of the Holy Spirit.

Remember that cutting words can never be recovered, so don't let harshness or verbal abuse be named among your character traits. Make a decision that kindness will be one of the core principles of your life.

TODAY'S AFFIRMATION:

I open my mouth with wisdom. The law of kindness is on my tongue.

Day 17

The Tactless Tongue

Let your conversation be gracious and effective so that you will have the right answer for everyone.

COLOSSIANS 4:6 NLT

Daniel and his three cohorts faced a real dilemma. Nebuchadnezzar, king of Babylon, had besieged their city and taken the inhabitants captive. He selected several handsome and intelligent young men of nobility who were to serve in his court once they completed a three-year training curriculum. The problem was that the king's nutritional program would require them to violate their strict kosher diet. Without any hint of rebelliousness, Daniel skillfully finessed his way out of his predicament.

> *Daniel purposed in his heart that he would not defile himself with the portion of the king's delicacies, nor with the wine which he drank; therefore he requested of the chief of*

> *the eunuchs that he might not defile him-*
> *self* (DANIEL 1:8 NKJV).

Notice that Daniel very tactfully *requested* permission to follow an alternative eating plan—even though he had already decided that under no circumstance was he going to partake of such defiled provisions. God gave him favor with the head training official, who agreed to let him follow a vegetarian diet. Lesson learned: We will always get more mileage from diplomacy than tactlessness.

I confess that being diplomatic is something I have to work at often. My direct, honest communication style has gotten me in more hot water than I care to admit. While honesty is indeed the best policy, it is not a license to say whatever we want. One of the most important skills we can develop is the ability to deal with others with sensitivity and to speak inoffensively when we find ourselves in difficult or problematic situations.

You would think that exhibiting graciousness would be an easy task for one who claims to be filled with the grace of God. Sometimes our lack of graciousness results from the communication styles we saw modeled when we were children. One of the people who influenced my life the most was an indirect communicator who tolerated the harsh words directed her way. Consequently, people often took advantage of her kind manner. I swore I would never be so tentative in my communication and would strive to be extremely clear in saying what I meant and meaning what I said. The Holy Spirit continues to bring balance in this area as I have acknowledged and repented of this emotional baggage. I am fully persuaded that only the grace of God can empower me to trash it.

Is it ever necessary to be brutally honest? After all, can't we be honest without being brutal? Even Job declared in the midst of his suffering, "How painful are honest words!" (JOB 6:25). Must pain always accompany the truth? The extent to which a person experiences pain from being told the truth depends on numerous variables, including his degree of emotional security, his perceived worth, or his desire to grow.

We must understand that extending grace and telling the truth are not mutually exclusive concepts. We can tell the truth tactfully. "For the law was given through Moses; grace and truth came through Jesus Christ" (JOHN 1:17). Jesus never allowed His graciousness to prevent Him from imparting the truth.

What about mean-spirited truthfulness? Have you ever been intentionally tactless? I have. However, when I have reflected on the situation later, I realized that even though I spoke words of truth, at the root of my actions were anger, frustration, disappointment, or retaliation. It was William Blake who said, "A truth that's told with bad intent beats all the lies you can invent." Of course, it is understood that we must always be quick to apologize for our intentional and unintentional tactlessness.

The key is to develop a habit of being tactful in every situation. I heard a story about a woman who went on a business trip and left her husband, Tom, with the responsibility of taking care of their cat and her live-in mother. She called home daily to see how things were going. After the third day, Tom informed her that the cat had eased out of the house a couple of days earlier and managed to climb onto the roof. He had tried in vain for several hours to coax him down. Frightened, the cat had jumped and sustained serious injury. The local veterinarian was doing all that he could for him. Filled with anxiety, the woman called the next day to get a status report on her beloved Mimi. Her husband, without finesse or feeling, simply told her, "The cat is dead." She was appalled at his insensitivity. She had to confront it. "I can't believe you are so tactless! When I called the first day, you could have said, 'Honey, the cat is on the roof.' The second day you could have said, 'The cat is at the vet and things aren't looking too good.' Today you could have said, 'Honey, our cat died. I'm so sorry.' You are impossible!" Having expressed her frustration, she calmly inquired, "By the way, how is Mother?" Tom slowly responded, "She's on the roof…"

Yes, becoming a tactful person does indeed require some practice. And like Tom, we may not bat a thousand right away. When we find ourselves about to say something tactless, however, we can do what the Federal Communications Commission sometimes mandates broadcasters to do—delay transmission. We can review the words in our minds and evaluate their impact. We can then choose to yield to the Holy Spirit's leading. This practice alone will help us to develop the emotional discipline necessary for stifling tactless remarks.

TODAY'S AFFIRMATION:

My words are seasoned with grace as I speak the truth in love.

Day 18

The Intimidating Tongue

The Philistine said to David, "Come to me, and I will give your flesh to the birds of the air and the beasts of the field!"

1 SAMUEL 17:44 NKJV

Goliath thought killing David was going to be a piece of cake since David was such an inexperienced warrior. Notwithstanding, Goliath decided to employ a little verbal intimidation before he triumphed over him. He engaged in name-calling, used threatening language, and tried to minimize David's potential— all standard tactics for the effective intimidator. David's response was not at all what Goliath expected. Rather than succumbing to fear, he assertively declared his faith in his God.

> *David said to the Philistine, "You come against me with sword and spear and javelin, but I come against you in the name of the LORD Almighty, the God of the armies*

of Israel, whom you have defied. This day
the LORD will hand you over to me, and I'll
strike you down and cut off your head"
(1 SAMUEL 17:45-46).

The intimidator counts on his victim to wilt in
the face of a verbal attack. That's why sometimes
(when it is safe) you have to let an intimidator know
you refuse to be oppressed by him and that you do
indeed have the God-given strength to resist his tactics. I worked on a major project once with a construction manager who attempted to intimidate
almost everyone involved by yelling at them. He
would often become belligerent during key negoti-
ations. His tactics worked on most of the subcon-
tractors and other workers. One day he decided to
target me for one of his tirades. He yelled like a
spoiled baby who had lost his pacifier. I waited
patiently while he ranted. When he finished, I calmly
responded, "I suppose I should let you know that
your yelling has absolutely no impact on me. I don't
know anybody who can intimidate me. God is the
only one I will ever fear." Even though he continued
to be a test to my patience during the rest of the
project, he soon learned that his intimidating style
was not going to advance his ball down my court,
especially since I was the one controlling payments

to everyone, including him! While it may be scary to confront intimidating bullies, they will often quickly back down when someone stands up to them.

God has never meant for anyone to oppress or dominate another person. Note that in the Garden of Eden, He gave Adam and Eve dominion over the fish, fowl, and animals—not over each other or other people.

> *God blessed them and said to them, "Be fruitful and increase in number; fill the earth and subdue it. Rule over the fish of the sea and the birds of the air and over every living creature that moves on the ground"* (GENESIS 1:28).

Although it can be a precursor to—but usually stops short of—physical violence, verbal intimidation can have a severe physical and emotional impact on its target. Many victims suffer from headaches, anxiety, nervousness, insomnia, stress, fatigue, low self-esteem, and depression. This is not how God intended His children to affect each other's lives.

Intimidators would do well to understand that their communication style only engenders resentment and subtle rebellion. They must learn that people are more inspired to connect with someone who will support them in their weaknesses. I marvel at the outpouring of support for Joel Osteen, who assumed the pastorate of Lakewood Church in Houston, Texas, after the death of his father. He had only worked in the media department of the church and had never preached before. Suddenly, he found himself thrust into the awesome task of leading a well-established, nationally recognized ministry. Rather than coming in like the new sheriff in town, he humbly accepted his new position, asked for the support and prayers of the congregation, and now has the one of the largest churches and television broadcasts in the United States. I have even heard nonchurchgoers speak of their admiration and support for him.

If you are an intimidator, it is time to get in touch with why you feel you need to gain power or control over others. You may need a good professional counselor to help you get to the root cause. Many intimidators grew up in chaotic or otherwise negative environments in which they felt powerless to change their circumstances. They vowed they would never allow their lives to be so out of control again, so they seek control. Others are simply a bundle of insecurities and use intimidation as a façade to mask their fears. Whatever the cause, intimidators can never hope to have a meaningful relationship with anyone who is forced into submission.

> ### TODAY'S AFFIRMATION:
>
> Because God is in control of every aspect of my life and has set my destiny, I have no need to control the behavior of others.

Day 19

The Rude Tongue

There will be a highway called the Holy Road.
No one rude or rebellious is permitted on this road.
It's for God's people exclusively.
ISAIAH 35:8 MSG

Speaking of the highway, wouldn't it be great if there were a special freeway for only nice, considerate people? The thoroughfares are the theater where road rage is played out every single day. Discourteous drivers yell obscenities to fellow drivers young and old.

What has made us so rude? Is it the overbooked schedules, longer commuting times, demanding bosses, spoiled children, and the stress of daily living? Perhaps our lack of patience can be attributed to the modern conveniences that allow us to do almost everything in mere seconds. Showing patience is a rare occurrence. Ill-mannered, discourteous communication has become standard practice—even among God's children. I was in a meeting recently where a man was attempting to make his point. He droned on in his normally slow and deliberate manner. A woman, frustrated with his pace, anxious about her next meeting, and lacking the grace to hold her thought until he finished, interrupted him. She finished his statement and completely changed the subject. The other members of the group looked uncomfortably at each other, but no one said anything—not even the man. Incidentally, it was a meeting of executives at a Christian organization.

Being rude to others is very denigrating to them and can spoil their entire day. Whatever happened to the Golden Rule? "Do to others as you would have them do to you" (LUKE 6:31). Do unto others? Why, we do not even have time to think about others! We are totally absorbed with our own agendas. Many of us can be counted among cell phone users who parade around public places talking at the top of their voices as if no one else is present. Just tonight at church, during a very critical moment, a woman sitting near the front of the sanctuary received a call on her cell phone, which rang loudly and several times before she answered it. My husband was appalled that she not only had the phone on in church but that she actually took the call. Cell phone users seem to be totally oblivious to their annoying and offensive social misconduct. And, even though some speak quietly, I have noticed people dining with others while spending an inordinate amount of time talking on the phone. It is no wonder that many relationships are so shallow these days.

Speaking of additional acts of rudeness, what about the cashiers at the checkout stands who are so engaged in their conversations with each other that they never offer a "hello"? That is so rude. And let's not forget the executive who takes phone calls during a meeting. This is disruptive and disrespectful.

Shouldn't our love for God and the desire to represent Him well here on earth have an impact on our day-to-day behavior? "Love is patient and kind. Love is not...rude. Love does not demand its own way" (1 CORINTHIANS 13:4-5 NLT).

What if someone is rude to us? Should we just let it go? Is it biblical to address the situation or should we just grin and bear it? While God has not called us to be a wimpy milquetoast who always rolls over and accepts rude behavior, we must confront rudeness in a direct but nonoffensive manner. It may not be necessary to tell a person, "You are so rude." However, it is a good idea to let her know you are aware of her lack of graciousness at the moment. Sometimes a well-phrased, caring question will do the trick. "Tough day, huh?" Of course, if you really feel that you have been mistreated, you should report the incident to someone in authority where possible. Some people continue their rudeness because they get away with it; reporting it may bring consequences that will ultimately change their behavior. Most importantly, do not allow people to suck you into the vacuum of their negativity by matching their rudeness with rudeness. The other day someone hung up in my face. My first thought was to call him back immediately so that I could return the behavior. The Holy Spirit reminded me of the admonitions I had written under the "Retaliating Tongue." There is never a justification for being rude.

If you find you tend to speak rudely to others, repent and recommit to following the Golden Rule. Know that when you are rude, you have made a very selfish and ungodly decision that your needs or concerns are paramount to all others.

God's people are patient, considerate, and kind. Remember that tomorrow when you encounter a person whose actions beg you to respond in an ungodly way.

> ——— TODAY'S AFFIRMATION: ———
>
> I will slow down and take the time to do unto others as I would have them do unto me.

Day 20

The Judgmental Tongue

Do not judge, or you too will be judged. For in the
same way you judge others, you will be judged.

MATTHEW 7:1-2

Jesus had no tolerance for those judgmental Pharisees. What a miserable bunch they were! This religious sect of the Jews was always looking for something to nitpick about regarding violation of the law of Moses or their own man-made traditions. Their critiquing ran the gamut from judging the disciples for not washing their hands to criticizing Jesus for healing on the Sabbath. Consider Jesus' response to them:

> *You judge by human standards; I pass judgment on no one. But if I do judge, my decisions are right, because I am not alone. I stand with the Father, who sent me* (JOHN 8:15-16).

Judgmental people engage in a critical, fault-finding assessment of another person's behavior. What is amazing is that they judge others by their *actions* but judge themselves by their *intentions*. Of course, most of us tend to judge others from an auto-biographical viewpoint. If someone's behavior does not reflect a choice or decision we would have made, we judge it as wrong. I often catch myself judging people who move at a slow pace as lazy or slow-witted—simply because the only two modes in which I operate are "intense" and "off." I have to remind myself that they are not lazy but just different.

There are some people who pass judgment on others based solely upon rumors they may have heard that may not have a modicum of truth. Benjamin Franklin, one of America's Founding Fathers, said, "I will speak ill of no man, not even in the matter of truth, but rather excuse the faults I hear, and, upon proper occasions, speak all the good I know of everybody." His philosophy follows the age-old parental advice: "If you can't say something nice, don't say anything at all."

We must be careful how we discuss others. My husband and I were members of a popular church which God eventually led us to leave. There had been many rumors circulating about the pastor. As inner circle leaders, we had indeed been privy to the details of some of the situations being discussed. However, we agreed it would serve no purpose to talk about these matters with others. It was interesting to note the disappointed looks on the faces of various members when they would engage us in conversation, only to find that we were not going to offer any information they could use to pass judgment on the pastor. Jesus was emphatic about His displeasure with judgmental folks.

> *Why do you look at the speck of sawdust in your brother's eye and pay no attention to the plank in your own eye? How can you say to your brother, "Let me take the speck out of your eye," when all the time there is a plank in your own eye? You hypocrite, first take the plank out of your own eye, and then you will see clearly to remove the speck from your brother's eye* (MATTHEW 7:3-5).

Jesus based His judgment of people's behavior on nothing other than God's standard. This is the only basis from which we can righteously judge. We would do well to focus more on judging ourselves than hunting for specks in the matters of others.

Pray for those whom you observe walking contrary to God's standards—but avoid judgment. If you have a genuine concern for someone and have earned the right to address his or her behavior, then do so in the spirit of love. Remember that you earn the right by consistently demonstrating your care and support.

TODAY'S AFFIRMATION:

I do not judge others or I too will be judged. For in the same way that I judge, I will be judged.

Day 21

The Self-Absorbed Tongue

Each of you should look not only to your own
interests, but also to the interests of others.

PHILIPPIANS 2:4

Haman, a Persian government official mentioned
in the book of Esther, was self-absorption personi-
fied. "Haman boasted to [his friends and wife] about
his vast wealth, his many sons, and all the ways the
king had honored him and how he had elevated him
above the other nobles and officials" (ESTHER 5:11).
On and on he went. Throughout the entire account
of his life, we never see him express interest in anyone
other than himself. Like Haman's family and friends,
some people perpetuate this kind of insensitivity by
grinning and bearing it, though they may be ever so
bored.

Are most of your conversations with others cen-
tered on you and your issues? A self-absorbed tongue

will surely alienate others as almost everyone desires to be the focus of attention occasionally.

I had an acquaintance with whom I spoke regularly with the hope of mutually sharing our individual concerns. It didn't take long before I realized that there was nothing mutual about our exchange. The minute I would mention one of my personal concerns, she would immediately identify with it through her own experience and suddenly the focus of the discussion was all about her. This happened time after time. I found this very frustrating as I never felt that I had the opportunity to share my issues. A few times I gently told her, "I really need you to listen to me right now." Trying to have a close relationship with a self-absorbed person is like trying to hug a porcupine.

Become aware of this character flaw in your communication. Ask God to make you genuinely interested in others. My friend Frank Wilson, who wrote or produced numerous gold albums for Motown Records before devoting his life to God, is such a person. He can talk to someone for an extended time and maintain a genuine interest in him. Despite his many accomplishments, he never seems to find a reason to inform his hearers of them. I have watched him interact with people of various economic and social levels. Without allowing his eyes to dart around the room looking for a more important person to engage, he focuses on the person at hand. Every part of him appears to say, "I am interested in what you are telling me." People love being in his presence.

If you find yourself involved with a self-absorbed person, try asking him to give you some advice or input about an issue that does not involve him. If he attempts to direct the conversation to himself, quickly acknowledge his concern about the matter but change the subject to something that is not about him. For instance, you may say, "I'm sure that this issue really concerns you. Did you hear about...?" If he persists, you would do well to muster the courage to say, "I really don't want to talk about that today." You may need to be a broken record as you attempt these strategies. After all, self-absorption dies hard.

If you admit to being the self-absorbed type, turn your desires for attention, ego boosting, and other selfish needs over to your Heavenly Shepherd, who supplies all your needs. Make a conscientious effort to become "others-absorbed." Challenge yourself to go a whole day or more without making your issues the focus of your communication. Give everyone you converse with your full attention, and watch your relationships deepen.

TODAY'S AFFIRMATION:

I look not only to my own interests, but to the interest of others. Therefore, my issues are not the primary topic of my conversations.

Day 22

The Cursing Tongue

*Out of the same mouth proceed
blessing and cursing. My brethren,
these things ought not to be so.*

JAMES 3:10 NKJV

Evie, an avowed Christian, faithfully attends prayer services, visits shut-ins, fasts for extended periods, and goes through all of the motions of being a Christian. However, she regularly uses four-letter words in her conversations. When a fellow Christian coworker confronted her about her use of such non-glorifying expressions, she responded, "These words are in the Bible." I have heard others snicker about her hypocrisy behind her back. Why does Evie use expletives as freely as she drinks water? Because she has not allowed the Holy Spirit to tame her tongue. James, the brother of Jesus, explained it this way:

> *No man can tame the tongue. It is an unruly*
> *evil, full of deadly poison. With it we bless*
> *our God and Father, and with it we curse*
> *men, who have been made in the similitude*
> *of God* (JAMES 3:8-9 NKJV).

Using profane, obscene, or vulgar language is unbecoming to a child of God. I believe people use profanity for various reasons. First, they often lack an adequate vocabulary with which to express themselves and therefore feel they must curse for their words to have impact. Those who are challenged in this area must start to develop a communication style that is direct, clear, and without hostility. They may find that expletives are unnecessary. Secondly, some people resort to profanity to release their extreme frustration with a situation. They have developed an ungodly pattern of expressing their displeasure and need to retrain their responses. They would do well to decide in advance upon some alternate words to use when they find themselves reaching the peak of frustration.

While I wholeheartedly believe that profane words should not come out of my mouth, I often found myself *thinking,* though not *saying,* them on many occasions. When I would stub my toe, break something of value, upset a stack of papers, spill a drink, have an encounter with an extremely difficult person, or confront any other frustrating situation, I would silently use profanity. I was quite troubled, especially as a Bible teacher, that such words came to my mind in these situations rather than an exclamation such as "Glory" or some other God-honoring phrase. I took the matter to the Lord in prayer. "Lord, I understand according to Luke 6:45, 'A good person produces good deeds from a good heart, and an evil person produces evil deeds from an evil heart. Whatever is in your heart determines what you say' (NLT). Would You please take the four-letter words out of my heart and replace them with Your expressions? I thank You in advance for purging me of profanity and for allowing the words of my mouth and the meditation of my heart to be acceptable in Your sight."

Understanding that profanity resides in the heart helps us to reject the idea that a curse word "slipped" out of our mouth. The reality is that it slipped out of the heart. Only God can cleanse a person's heart. If you are challenged with profanity, ask God to purify your heart and your mind. Remember that words are verbal thoughts. We must practice the mental discipline of casting down profane thoughts

and using words that bring life to our innermost
being and to others.

---- TODAY'S AFFIRMATION: ----

Cursing does not proceed out of my
mouth. Today I give God full charge
of my tongue. By His grace I will only
speak words that will bring honor to
His name.

Day 23

The Complaining Tongue

I cry aloud with my voice to the LORD;
I make supplication with my voice to the LORD.
I pour out my complaint before Him;
I declare my trouble before Him.

PSALM 142:1-2 NASB

The five daughters of Zelophehad had a problem.
Their father had died in the wilderness before the
Israelites came into the Promised Land. Zelophehad
did not have any sons to inherit his portion of the
land, and the law did not provide for women to
receive the son's portion instead. Consequently, his
daughters, not having a father, brother, husband, son,
or any other man in their immediate family, were left
out completely. Rather than complaining to others,
they called a "congressional hearing" (NUMBERS 27)
and presented their petition for an inheritance to
Moses and the leaders. When Moses took their case
to God, He agreed with the women and granted their

97

request. Now, what do you think the outcome would have been had they simply whined to anyone in the multitude who would listen rather than bringing it to those in authority? I doubt they would have obtained their inheritance.

A legitimate complaint can only be resolved if you direct it to the one who can change your situation. Only a few people who are dissatisfied, annoyed, or upset by an experience actually take steps to officially complain about it. They prefer to waste time soliciting others to commiserate with them. What an exercise in futility. Not only could their input to the right person improve things for them but for others as well. For example, on several occasions I find myself in a store where the line is growing longer by the minute. Rather than joining the other customers who are whining about the situation, I seek out (sometimes yell for) the store manager and ask him to open another register. Most of the time this works.

The psalmist in the opening Scripture of this chapter did not bore, frustrate, or waste the time of others with his complaints. He declares, "I pour out my complaint before Him," the one who could bring change.

Notwithstanding, even God tires of constant complaints.

Someone once said, "To swear is wicked because it is taking God's name in vain. To murmur is likewise wicked, for it takes God's promises in vain." During your tongue fast, become aware of how often you complain about nonessential matters such as a rainy day, traffic jams, boring television programs, lazy coworkers, and so on.

Because complaining is contagious, this is a hard mouth malady to cure. In the past I have found myself joining in with complaining wives just to have something in common with them, even though my husband was not guilty of the things about which they complained. I knew I risked envy and alienation if I confessed to what a wonderful, supportive man he is. Sometimes I would try to search for something to whine about and would come up with something as shallow as the fact that he eats several times a day. The man maintains a proper weight and makes his own food most of the time! What is there to complain about except that I resent his metabolism?

If you are a complainer, you must start to resist the constant "ain't it awful" party. Trust me, others will be glad you did and will stop dreading conversations with you. This is not to say you shouldn't seek an occasional sympathetic ear or wise counsel from a valued source. However, if you are going to ignore their advice and continue to rehearse the problem each time you converse, beware. Thy listener shall soon become weary of thee! Whenever you feel a complaint coming on, replace it with a statement of gratitude or a declaration of a Scripture you have personalized.

—— TODAY'S AFFIRMATION: ——

Because God works all things together for my good, according to His purpose for my life, I will not complain.

Day 24

The Retaliating Tongue

Don't repay evil for evil. Don't retaliate when
people say unkind things about you. Instead,
pay them back with a blessing. That is what God
wants you to do, and he will bless you for it.
1 PETER 3:9 NLT

There is nothing as easy as verbal retaliation. Of course, the thrill of it is only a fleeting pleasure for those who love God; the remorse for succumbing to this sin tends to linger. Retaliation used to be one of my biggest challenges. That's why I praise God for His Holy Spirit who convicts, guides, and works in me to do His good pleasure. I have made a concerted effort in recent months to take the high road in every situation in which someone attempts to criticize, diminish, or disparage me in any way. I knew I would not be able to write this chapter if I did not get the victory over this stronghold.

Satan has presented me with many opportunities to practice my desired behavior. While I do not recall an instance of returning a negative response directly to someone, I found pleasure in sharing with my administrative assistant, my husband, or a friend the words that I would have said had I not chosen the high road. The Holy Spirit impressed upon me that this was still my way of getting indirect satisfaction. The ultimate victory would come only when I refused to dignify the person's remarks with any comments and refrained from discussing the matter with anyone. Satan has taunted me and tried to make me feel that I am becoming a wimp. You would have to know how much I loath people who let others treat them like a doormat to really understand how hard this has been for me. I grew up seeing key people in my life suffer the harsh words of others in silence. I promised myself that if anybody treated me that way, I would return the treatment. However, as I studied the Scriptures dealing with conflict management, I learned that the root meaning of the word "retaliate" is to "return the punishment." The Bible is very clear in admonishing us to avoid retaliation.

> *Never pay back evil for evil to anyone. Do things in such a way that everyone can see you are honorable. Do your part to live in*

> *peace with everyone, as much as possible.*
> *Dear friends, never avenge yourselves.*
> *Leave that to God. For it is written, "I will*
> *take vengeance; I will repay those who*
> *deserve it," says the Lord* (ROMANS 12:17-
> 19 NLT).

I suspect I will not always bat a thousand in this area in every situation; however, I know that if I strike out, it will be because I have ignored the urging of the Holy Spirit and made a conscious decision to take God's job by returning the punishment. In recalling those times when I have been victorious, I realize that my responses required humility, a desire to understand the other person's behavior, and a commitment to obey and glorify God.

To reinforce my ongoing commitment not to retaliate, I sometimes declare a "Jesus" day and make every effort on that day to do what Jesus would do and to say what He would say. Now, I know that this should be my lifestyle as a child of God. However, the practicality of it hits home when I take it a day at a time. I encourage you to take up this challenge and see yourself grow ten feet tall in the spirit. Try to stay mindful of the fact that when we decide that it is our personal responsibility to avenge the wrongs perpetrated against us, we have crossed the boundary into forbidden territory.

> ## TODAY'S AFFIRMATION:
>
> I will not repay evil with evil or insult with insult, but with blessing, because to this I have been called so that I may inherit a blessing.

Day 25

The Accusing Tongue

The accuser of our brothers,
who accuses them before our God day
and night, has been hurled down.

REVELATION 12:10

Things were going badly for Job. He had lost his children, his health, and his wealth. To add insult to injury, his insensitive, well-meaning friends accused him of pride, covetousness, and a host of other character failings (JOB 22). Although they came to sympathize with him, these three miserable comforters spent the majority of the time trying to convince Job he was responsible for his own woes. Such an accusation was more than this innocent victim of satanic circumstances could bear. Job knew he was an upright man who walked in complete integrity. Wracked with physical pain, he was also forced to bear the pain of false accusations.

Have you ever charged someone with wrong-doing before you established evidence of his guilt? When you do so, you fall into the same pattern as Satan, the official accuser of God's children.

Emotional and spiritual maturity dictate that you must seek first to understand rather than making an accusation. Look at the example God set in the Garden of Eden when Adam and Eve blew it. He could have easily said, "Adam and Eve, you ungrateful sinners, I should never have trusted you in My garden!" God's non-accusatory style in confronting Adam and Eve about their trespass provides a powerful model for those of us who tend to accuse before obtaining all the facts of the matter.

> *Then the LORD God called to Adam and said to him, "Where are you?" So he said, "I heard Your voice in the garden, and I was afraid because I was naked; and I hid myself." And He said, "Who told you that you were naked? Have you eaten from the tree of which I commanded you that you should not eat?"* (GENESIS 3:9-11 NKJV).

I could not help but note that God already knew the answer to each of the three questions He asked Adam. Notwithstanding, He gave Adam an opportunity to explain his behavior. Asking a clarifying question and listening to the response are key steps in overcoming an accusing tongue. I repeat, ask, and listen.

Has anyone ever accused you falsely? Have your motives been called into question when you knew they were pure? How should you respond to such injustice? Well, the first step is to ask God's guidance as to whether to proclaim your innocence and the best way to do so. If the lie has affected someone, you might explain to that person that the accusation is simply not true. You have no control over whether or not he will believe you. Also, if you are not certain who the perpetrator is, do not waste your energy trying to find the source of the lie. Know that all lies originate with Satan. Period.

I have had people make comments about another person's incompetence or shortcomings and then falsely attribute their statement to me to give it credibility. When I have opportunity to refute an accusation, I will do so. If not, I simply ask God to bring the truth to light. I cannot afford to divert my mental energies away from worthwhile projects to chase feathers that have been loosed to the wind. God is my vindicator, and He will do a much better job than I ever could do in seeing that justice is done.

TODAY'S AFFIRMATION:

With God's help, today I will tune my ears to wisdom and concentrate on understanding. I will cry out for insight and understanding. I will search for them as I would for lost money or hidden treasure.

Day 26

The Discouraging Tongue

When they were discouraged, I smiled at them.
My look of approval was precious to them.
JOB 29:24 NLT

Have you ever dampened someone's hope, confidence, or enthusiasm by raising objections to his proposed action? An untold number of individuals have missed their destiny because of someone's discouraging words. Teachers have dashed the dreams of students who had mediocre grades or other shortcomings. Would-be inventors abandoned their pursuit of innovative ideas once family members and society ridiculed them. I do not believe that people who have dissuaded others in such a manner deliberately intended to discourage them, but rather spoke out of their own lack of faith in God's ability to "do exceeding abundantly above all that we ask or think, according to the power that works in us" (EPHESIANS 3:20 NKJV).

Discouragement has wreaked havoc for ages. Consider the Israelites and their quest for the Promised Land. Right at the brink of reaching their destination, Moses sent Joshua and Caleb along with ten other leaders on a 40-day exploration of Canaan, a land flowing with milk and honey. There they saw everything in extreme abundance. The size of the fruit surpassed anything you would ever see at the county fair. Why, it took two men to carry a cluster of grapes! They also noted something else unusual—giant-sized men. When they reported back to Moses and the multitude, Joshua and Caleb encouraged the Israelites to proceed to conquer the land. Their cohorts, however, had a different perspective.

> *The other men who had explored the land with him answered, "We can't go up against them! They are stronger than we are!" So they spread discouraging reports about the land among the Israelites: "The land we explored will swallow up any who go to live there. All the people we saw were huge. We even saw giants there, the descendants of Anak. We felt like grasshoppers next to them, and that's what we looked like to them!"* (NUMBERS 13:31-33 NLT).

Despite all of the miracles that they had witnessed God perform on their behalf, the multitude believed the discouraging report. They talked of returning to Egypt and even wanted to stone Joshua and Caleb for their optimism. God's punishment for their unbelief was swift and severe.

> Then the ten scouts who had incited the rebellion against the LORD by spreading discouraging reports about the land were struck dead with a plague before the LORD. Of the twelve who had explored the land, only Joshua and Caleb remained alive (NUMBERS 14:36-38 NLT).

Not only did the Lord kill the discouragers, He forced the entire multitude to turn back and to wander in the wilderness for 40 years. Further, God forbade all of those—except Caleb and Joshua—who were more than 20 years of age at that time to enter the Promised Land; they all died in the wilderness. The discouraging words of ten men caused thousands of men and women to miss their inheritance. If only the ten had chosen to be encouragers instead!

What about you? When you see others faced with negative circumstances, do you lose hope in their ability to succeed? Further, can you listen to someone's dreams and plans without making disheartening remarks? This is not to say that you should not question the viability of an idea that seems to have no merit, nor fail to offer objective input to warn against potential failure. However, a well-phrased question can be much more effective than a straight out "That's impossible!" For example, asking a young entrepreneur, "How did you determine the market for your product?" sounds better than, "Gee, I don't think many people would be interested in that!"

Even if you cannot envision the dreams of another, at least agree to stand in faith with him for God's perfect will to be done regarding the proposed endeavor. Henry Ford once said that the ability to encourage others is one of life's biggest assets. Think of the people who have encouraged you during your lifetime and what a positive effect their words had on you. In a world plagued with negativity, everyone needs a little encouragement from time to time. Make a conscious effort to always speak sincere words of affirmation, support, and inspiration to those within your circle of concern.

If, perchance, you are confronted by a discourager, do not let him derail your destiny. Very graciously let him know your eyes are fixed on God, who specializes in doing the impossible. Better yet, be highly selective of those with whom you share your dreams. Their lack of initiative and faith, and even their envy, may very well cause you to abort your plans.

TODAY'S AFFIRMATION:

Worry weighs a person down; but my encouraging words will cheer him up.

Day 27

The Doubting Tongue

*For assuredly, I say to you, whoever says
to this mountain, "Be removed and be cast
into the sea," and does not doubt in his heart,
but believes that those things he says will be done,
he will have whatever he says.*

MARK 11:23 NKJV

I fought hard to resist the knots that were attempting to form in the pit of my stomach. This was my first flight since the September 11, 2001, terrorist attacks on America. Though tempted, I refrained from expressing my fear to the passenger in the seat next to me.

As the plane taxied down the runway, I started to audibly quote various portions of Psalm 91: "This I declare of the LORD: He alone is my refuge, my place of safety; He is my God, and I am trusting Him (VERSE 2)…Do not be afraid of the terrors of the night, nor fear the dangers of the day (VERSE 5)…

Though a thousand fall at your side, though ten thousand are dying around you, these evils will not touch you (VERSE 7)...For He orders his angels to protect you wherever you go (VERSE 11)" (NLT).

Long before the day of the flight, I had been confessing to myself and to everyone else that I was not afraid of flying again, but now I found myself at the point where the rubber literally met the road. The promises of Psalm 91, as always, proved to be my salvation. Over the years they had become the corner I ran to in fearful situations. As I heard myself repeating these verses, my apprehensions began to subside. I made a conscious decision to relax and to leave the flying to God. In my mind's eye I envisioned angels holding the tips of each wing of the plane. I found this visual especially helpful during a few moments of turbulence we experienced during the flight. Each time I declared, "His angels have orders to keep this plane safe." I arrived at my destination without incident. I had triumphed over doubt.

If we ever hope to tame a doubting tongue, we must become familiar with the promises of God. Words of doubt come out of an unbelieving heart. Of course, merely knowing the promises of God is not enough; we must become proficient at declaring them. Faith comes by hearing (ROMANS 10:17). The more we declare our unbelief, the more reinforced it becomes. The more we assert our confidence in a positive outcome, the more our faith increases. Because we will believe what we constantly hear, we must take personal responsibility for what we hear. We may have to limit—or eliminate—our contact with individuals who tend to express negativity about various outcomes, goals, or results we desire.

Often our words of doubt originate out of our tendency to act in self-confidence. Self-confidence is a concept touted by the world that tells us we must rely on our own skills and abilities. This is a direct contradiction to King Solomon's warning, "He who trusts in himself is a fool² (Proverbs 28:26). When we face a challenge and quickly assess our own ability to conquer it, we will most likely come up short— and doubting. We must be on guard not to give our doubts substance by declaring them.

If the spirit of unbelief plagues you, I challenge you to get a good study Bible and to search the Scriptures for verses relating to your areas of concern. Write down a passage, meditate on it often, and memorize it. I keep a template on my computer for typing Scriptures to fit a 5x7 picture frame. I will select a passage that is relevant to a current problem. I cut it out, frame it, and keep it before me on my desk until I solidify it in my heart. When doubts arise, I nail them with the selected Word of God. This sounds simple but is not easy. Some doubts die hard. We must be persistent in declaring our victory.

What are some things you find yourself speaking about in a doubtful way? Is it the fear of pursuing a career or task for which you feel inadequate? The hopelessness of forging an amicable relationship with a difficult person? The seemingly impossible task of getting into shape? Perhaps you have resorted to being a Doubting Thomas who would only believe what he could touch (see JOHN 20:25).

God's children are to live by faith—in God. We cannot afford to get stymied in the "sense realm" of what we can see and feel. Our doubts can deter our destiny.

Our attitudes and conversations will change when we face the reality that apart from God we can do absolutely nothing. Decide today to skip the skepticism, doubt the doubts, and believe the best!

TODAY'S AFFIRMATION:

Anything is possible for me if I believe. Therefore, I will declare my faith rather than discuss my doubts.

Day 28

The Loquacious Tongue

When words are many, sin is not absent,
but he who holds his tongue is wise.

PROVERBS 10:19

Have you ever talked to someone who seemed to have diarrhea of the mouth? On and on she goes, from one topic to another. Well, know from henceforth that the proper word for this malady is "loquaciousness." It's just a big word for a "motor mouth." While it is generally concluded that females have cornered the market on this use of the tongue, men can be guilty too. Now, I admit that I am not a "silent lamb" by any stretch of the imagination. In fact, my husband says that I will talk to a stop sign. However, I also take great pleasure in listening to others. In fact, people who are reputed to be shy talk to me freely.

When I am in the presence of an incessant talker, I often wonder if that person is lonely, has few opportunities to talk to others, or just plain loves the sound of her voice. Whatever the motivation, excessive talking tends not to glorify God. I heard someone say that any conversation that lasts more than ten minutes will usually end up on the wrong path. The apostle Paul admonished the Thessalonians to "study to be quiet" (1 THESSALONIANS 4:11 KJV). To "study" implies a striving or intense effort. It will take some work to overcome this entrenched habit.

Dr. Joe R. Brown of Rochester, Minnesota, tells of trying to get a physical history of a patient. The man's wife answered every question the doctor asked. Finally, Dr. Brown requested that she leave the room, but after she left he found that her husband couldn't speak. Calling the wife back, Dr. Brown apologized for not realizing the man had aphasia—loss of speech—and could not speak a word. The wife was astonished. She didn't know it either.*

If in the midst of your conversation you find yourself veering down the path of loquaciousness, try these quick detours:

- Simply stop talking and ask the other person an open-ended question that would cause him to respond with more than a simple yes or no. For example, "John, what do you think about…?"

---

* P.L. Tan, *Encyclopedia of 7700 Illustrations* (Garland, TX: Bible Communications, 1979, 1996).

- Make the talking count. My mentor, the late Dr. Juanita Smith, would often say, "I am not a woman of few words, but I love to talk about the things of God." Share an interesting news story you've heard or an insight God has given you on a Scripture. For example, rather than succumbing to a negative conversation, I keep telling everyone about my "tongue fast" and the truths God has revealed from His Word during my search of the Scriptures. They listen with great interest and benefit.

--- TODAY'S AFFIRMATION: ---

When my words are many, sin is not absent, but when I hold my tongue, I am considered wise.

Day 29

The Indiscreet Tongue

Discretion will protect you,
and understanding will guard you.

PROVERBS 2:11

After the great flood that destroyed most of the earth, Noah planted a vineyard. One day he got carried away and drank too much wine. His son Ham discovered him in his tent—drunk and naked. Scripture tells us that Ham "saw his father's nakedness and told his two brothers outside" (GENESIS 9:22). Exercising more discretion than Ham, his brothers would not even look on their father, but backed into the tent and covered him with a garment. Their discretion was a sign of their maturity. One who is discreet shows prudence and wise self-restraint in speech and behavior—and always reaps a positive consequence.

Indiscretion can be costly. Some subject matters should simply be off limits for discussion. You would be wise to never discuss your salary or bonus—especially with other company personnel. Your sex life should also be off limits as an item of discussion with a non-counseling outsider.

Ham's indiscretion proved costly. When Noah sobered up, he realized his shame and was sorely displeased with the manner in which Ham had handled the situation.

Have you ever found out something about a leader or other prominent person and could not refrain from telling someone? If God has trusted you enough to reveal someone's nakedness or sin, have you ever considered that you were not to "see" and "tell" but rather to cover that nakedness with discretion and intercession?

Having grown up in church, I have seen the nakedness of many leaders. God has often reminded me that He was trusting me not to "cover up," but to "cover with." It can be a very uncomfortable position. God may even call you to confront the individual regarding his or her wrongdoing. He did so with Nathan the prophet, who confronted David about his adultery with Bathsheba and his subsequent murder of her husband to cover it up (2 SAMUEL 12). Whatever God mandates, do it His way. A public revelation is not always necessary as it can cause irreparable damage to the body of Christ. David's sin with Bathsheba never became the topic of a public scandal. However, David suffered the consequences through his family and other areas of his life. A leader's punishment is God's business.

Caution! If you serve in a position of authority, such as a member of a board of directors, then you have a responsibility to deal with ungodly behavior in a leader. Confront with love and compassion. No one is perfect, and no one has 20-20 vision on himself. Remember that. God may someday show someone your nakedness. Pray that it will be handled with wisdom. Plant the seed of discretion now.

TODAY'S AFFIRMATION:

My discretion will protect me and understanding will guard me.

Day 30

The Silent Tongue

There is a time for everything,
and a season for every activity under heaven...
a time to be silent and a time to speak.

ECCLESIASTES 3:1,7

I heard a story about a husband and wife who were feuding and giving each other the silent treatment. One night he realized he needed her to wake him up at an early hour to catch a flight. Not wanting to humble himself and be the first to break the silence, he left her a note to wake him at 5 A.M. The next morning he awakened to find out that he had overslept by a couple of hours and had missed his flight. As he leaped out of bed to go and angrily confront her, he noticed a piece of paper on his nightstand. The note read, "It is 5 A.M. Wake up!"

Not all silence is golden. I have devoted the previous chapters to encourage you to abstain from various negative uses of the tongue. By now you may have concluded you will never be able to say more than a few words for the rest of your life if you are to tame the little unruly member that sets the course of your destiny. If you have decided a vow of silence is your only hope, read on.

Talking is absolutely essential to maintaining effective relationships. As a child, your parents or teachers may have drilled into you the proverb that "silence is golden." The truth is that this is a half-quoted proverb. The complete saying is, "Speech is silver, silence is golden." While keeping one's mouth shut is a great virtue, effective communication is to a relationship what oxygen is to the body. To say "speech is silver" implies that speaking has significant value. Silver was once a primary medium of exchange, just as currency is today. It was used to trade one value for another. When we talk, it should be an exchange of valuable information. All the previous chapters of this book have highlighted various types of negative communications that provided no value. Let's now focus on those instances in which silence has no value.

Silence is not golden when one uses it as a passive, retaliatory means of expressing his anger or displeasure with a situation. In fact, such silence is a direct violation of our Lord's command to confront those who offend us.

> *Moreover if thy brother shall trespass against thee, go and tell him his fault between thee and him alone: if he shall hear thee, thou hast gained thy brother* (MATTHEW 18:15 KJV).

Jesus is recommending pretty assertive behavior in commanding us to take the initiative in addressing an offense or a trespass. Trespassing is an unauthorized crossing of a boundary. Many times we may feel we have been trespassed or wronged, but rather than discussing the issue with the offender, we resort to sulking and pouting. Women are especially prone to keeping silent as most have been socialized to think it is unladylike to be so direct as to say, "I was offended by your actions. Please don't do that again." Unfortunately, this lack of communication leaves many offenders totally unaware that their behavior has negatively affected us. Thus, they are more likely to repeat the offense.

Silence is not golden when we refuse to defend someone against unwarranted criticism or vicious rumors. We cannot let our fear of alienation or rejection cause us to allow slander and character assassinations when we are well aware of facts to the contrary. I recently found myself coming to the defense of a person who I knew had accused me falsely to several of my acquaintances. This could have been my opportunity to "pay her back," but I knew she was innocent of the charges being made. Without hesitation I told the accuser so. I felt that it made God smile.

Silence is not golden when it results in us making an undesirable decision by default. After all, silence can indicate consent. Prayer was taken out of public schools in the United States because the majority kept quiet and did not protest. In the book of Numbers, Moses reiterated that silence is indeed consent. He gave instructions on how to deal with single women who made vows:

> *When a young woman still living in her father's house makes a vow to the LORD or obligates herself by a pledge and her father hears about her vow or pledge but says nothing to her, then all her vows and every pledge by which she obligated herself will stand. But if her father forbids her when he hears about it, none of her vows or the pledges by which she obligated herself will stand; the LORD will release her because her father has forbidden her* (NUMBERS 30:3-5).

He went on to instruct in verses 10-15 that the same rules applied to a married woman. Her vow was to stand if her husband failed to protest it in a timely manner. His silence gave consent to her actions.

A Japanese proverb states, "Silent worms dig holes in the walls." To keep silent when one should be speaking is a sure way to dig holes in your relationships.

TODAY'S AFFIRMATION

I will not keep silent when I should be speaking.

Epilogue

Okay. You have finished reading this book, and it probably did not take 30 days to do so. The reading was just step one. Now you are ready to home in on areas where your mouth is particularly challenged. You may have to spend several days or weeks on the "Lying Tongue" and no time on the "Cursing Tongue." You may even decide to engage in a period of verbal abstinence for one day each week rather than 30 days straight. Whatever your strategy, I guarantee you that as you meditate on the Scriptures that address the ungodly uses of the tongue, you will become highly sensitive to the areas where you need God's grace and deliverance.

To assess your progress, daily review the tongue evaluation checklist in Appendix A. The list summarizes the 30 negative uses of the tongue we have discussed. When you can answer no to every question on a regular basis, you can rest assured that the Holy Spirit has gotten the upper hand on that little unruly member no man can tame. You are now ready to turn your attention from the negative uses of the tongue and turn it into a wellspring of life. Since it is more effective to focus on implementing positive behavior than trying to avoid the negative, Appendix B offers alternative uses of the tongue that will bring glory to God and improve your interactions and relationships with others. You are now free to engage in building others up, sharing knowledge and wisdom, exhorting, inspiring faith, confronting in love, and giving life to your hearers. To reinforce your commitment to a wholesome tongue and to have power for more positive proclamations, regularly meditate on the Scriptures in Appendix C, "Arsenal of Tongue Scriptures." The selected passages will fortify your inner man and revolutionize your conversations. Continue to decree that the words of your mouth have become acceptable in the sight of the Lord. Finally, act as if the words you speak will become your personal reality. They will!

The Power of Words

A careless word may kindle strife;
A cruel word may wreck a life.
A bitter word may hate instill;
A brutal word may smite and kill.
A gracious word may smooth the way;
A joyous word may light the day.
A timely word may lessen stress;
A loving word may heal and bless.

Author Unknown

Appendix A

DAILY TONGUE EVALUATION CHECKLIST

To measure your progress in taming your tongue, ask yourself the following questions at the end of each day. On a separate sheet, note the number of Yes's.

___ Did I engage in any form of lying?

___ Did I flatter someone?

___ Did I manipulate someone for my gain or advantage?

___ Did I speak too hastily?

___ Did my words cause division?

___ Was I argumentative or contentious?

___ Did I boast or speak with pride?

___ Did I engage in a self put-down?

___ Did I slander someone?

___ Did I gossip?

___ Did I meddle in anybody's affairs?

___ Did I betray someone's trust?

___ Did I belittle someone?

___ Was I cynical, scornful, or sarcastic?

___ Did I speak as a Know-It-All?

___ Did I use harsh or abusive words?

___ Did I fail to speak with tact or diplomacy?

___ Did I attempt to intimidate with my words?

___ Was I rude?

___ Was I critical or judgmental?

___ Was I self-absorbed in my conversations?

___ Did I use profanity?

___ Did I complain?

___ Did I retaliate?

___ Did I accuse someone?

___ Was I discouraging?

___ Did I express doubt and unbelief?

___ Did I simply talk too much?

___ Was I indiscreet in my discussions?

___ Did I keep silent when I should have communicated?

If you answered no to all of the questions above, rejoice—but do not relax. Quietly ask the Holy Spirit to show you your next focus area of spiritual development. Know that you will reach perfection only when you get to heaven.

Appendix B

ALTERNATIVE USES OF THE TONGUE

Having refrained from negative speaking, see how many positive ways you can engage your tongue in a single day. Use the list below for starters.

❏ Pray.

❏ Share your faith.

❏ Express gratitude.

❏ Tell the truth.

❏ Admit a mistake.

❏ Apologize.

❏ Confess your faults or weaknesses.

❏ Applaud someone's achievement.

❏ Ask for help.

❏ Offer to assist.

❏ Comfort someone who is hurting.

❏ Communicate your expectations.

❏ Give a sincere compliment.

❏ Confront an interpersonal conflict.

❏ Pledge your support.

❏ Defend someone against negative criticism.

❏ Discourage gossip.

❏ Express appreciation.

❏ Offer constructive feedback.

❏ Share your knowledge.

❏ Keep a secret.

❏ Protest evil.

❏ Put forth a new idea.

❏ Recite Scripture.

❏ Reconcile parties in conflict.

❏ Relate a meaningful story.

❏ Tell a clean joke.

❏ Express hope or optimism.

❏ Encourage someone to persevere.

❏ Express concern for another.

❏ Say "Please."

❏ Sing a song.

❏ Speak of God's goodness.

Appendix C

ARSENAL OF TONGUE SCRIPTURES

I will bless the LORD at all times: his praise shall continually be in my mouth.

PSALM 34:1 KJV

Let your speech be always with grace, seasoned with salt, that ye may know how ye ought to answer every man.

COLOSSIANS 4:6 KJV

My mouth will speak words of wisdom; the utterance from my heart will give understanding.

PSLAM 49:3

Do all things without complaining and disputing.

PHILIPPIANS 2:14 NKJV

Listen, for I have worthy things to say; I open my lips to speak what is right. My mouth speaks what is true, for my lips detest wickedness.

PROVERBS 8:6-7

For there is not a word in my tongue, but, lo, O LORD, thou knowest it altogether.

PSALM 139:4 KJV

Let my mouth be filled with thy praise and with thy honour all the day.

PSALM 71:8 KJV

The mouth of a righteous man is a well of life: but violence covereth the mouth of the wicked.

PROVERBS 10:11 KJV

The Lord GOD has given Me the tongue of the learned, that I should know how to speak a word in season to him who is weary. He awakens Me morning by morning, He awakens my ear to hear as the learned.

ISAIAH 50:4 NKJV

I said, "I will guard my ways, lest I sin with my tongue; I will restrain my mouth with a muzzle, while the wicked are before me."

PSALM 39:1 NKJV

Like apples of gold in settings of silver is a word spoken in right circumstances.

PROVERBS 25:11 NASB

You will also declare a thing, and it will be established for you; so light will shine on your ways.

JOB 22:28 NKJV

My tongue will speak of your righteousness and of your praises all day long.

PSALM 35:28

How to Contact the Author

Deborah Smith Pegues is an experienced certified public accountant, a Bible teacher, a speaker, a certified behavioral consultant specializing in understanding personality temperaments, and the author of *30 Days to Taming Your Tongue*. She and her husband, Darnell, have been married for more than 25 years and make their home in California.

For speaking engagements, please contact the author at:

The Pegues Group
P.O. Box 56382
Los Angeles, California 90056
(323) 293-5861
or
Email: ddpegues@sbcglobal.net
www.confrontingissues.com

Also by Deborah Smith Pegues at
www.confrontingissues.com:

Managing Conflict God's Way: Biblical Strategies for Effective Confrontations

"Show Me the Money!": Uncovering the Eight Pitfalls to Financial Freedom